AF267481

TABLE OF CONTENTS

EDITORIAL **6**
Page 5

NICOLLETTE SULLIVAN
Her sweet dreams are reviving
the goldent era of jazz

REVIEW **11**
Over-sexualization
of female artists

WOMEN'S HISTORY MONTH
-Women in the music industry
- Books about women
who changed the world
- Top women indie artists

STYLE **18**
- Spring 2021
must-have fashion

BEAUTY
Spring 2011
make-up trends

TOP TIPS **26**
Making a living
with your music

CINEMA
The United States Vs.
Billie Holiday

HUMANITARIAN AWARENESS
Women-led music organizations
you need to join

Pump it up
MAGAZINE

PUMP IT UP MAGAZINE ————

LINKS

WEBSITE
www.pumpitupmagazine.com

FACEBOOK
www.facebook.com/pumpitupmagazine

TWITTER
www.twitter.com/pumpitupmag

SOUNDCLOUD
www.soundcloud.com/pumpitupmagazine

INSTAGRAM
pumpitupmagazine

PINTEREST
www.pinterest.com/pumpitupmagazine

PUMP IT UP MAGAZINE
30721 Russell Ranch Road
Suite 140
Westlake Village,
California 91362
United States
www.pumpitupmagazine.com
info@pumpitupmagazine.com
Tel : (001) (877)841 – 7414 (toll free number)

Greetings readers,

Wow how time flies. Seems it was just yesterday and we were headed to the voting booth. Speaking of voting it was not that long ago (well, 1920) that women gained their right to vote and since then the contributions of women to events in history,are unsurpassed. This months edition of Pump It Up Magazine celebrates Women's History Month.

Our cover girl this month is the beautiful Nicollette Sullivan who's new single "Sweet Dreams" is moving up the charts. Not only is she beautiful, but intelligent and talented.

We have new music by two equally talented women , Sara Rose's "Love is Calling" and Em, who's single Say What You Mean is proving to be a bonafide smash! Now "Say What You Mean "The Remixes" are taking off as well.

When it comes to women in Gospel , Minister Phyllis McMeans solid track "Help" is a inspirational gem!

Last but not least , I am happy to announce the release of my first Smooth Jazz album in America. It's called "Satisfied" I hope you will like it.

So,flip through the pages of this edition and celebrate with us Women's History Month.

Oops! Don't for get to watch the critically acclaimed film " The United States vs Billie Holiday" and tune in to Pump It Up Magazine Radio where all the hits are played.

And a big Happy Birthday shout out to my mom who's been inspiration to me.

Be Safe and be blessed.

Anissa Boudjaoui

CONTRIBUTORS

EDITOR IN CHIEF
Anissa Boudjaoui

MUSIC
Michael B. Sutton

FASHION
Tiffani Sutton

MARKETING
Grace Rose
Corinne Reyes

PARTNERS

Editions L.A.
www.editions-la.com

The Sound Of L.A.
www.thesoundofla.com

Info Music
www.infomusic.fr

Delit Face
www.DelitFace.com

L.A. Unlimited
www.launlimitedinc.com

Nicollette Sullivan Photography by:

Adrian Jose Gonzalez
Page 8

Margaret Molloy
Page 6,7,9

Originally from Venice, California, singer and songwriter Nicollette Sullivan has dazzled audiences with her spellbinding talent and grace. Her unique musical perspective is shaped by influences like Billie Holiday, Etta James, Josephine Baker, Ella Fitzgerald, Nina Simone and the fusion of elements from Jazz, R&B, Blues, Gospel, and Pop music genres. Nicollette's distinct musical tastes have fueled a stunning new single, which is a cover of the synth-pop classic originally performed by the Eurythmics, titled Sweet Dreams.

Nicollette Sullivan is able to make Sweet Dreams her own with an inventive and equally seductive vocal performance that transforms the meaning of the song without even changing the tune's words. She is not only able to turn Sweet Dreams into something soulful but give the title a sense of personal charm

1. THANK YOU SO MUCH FOR TAKING THE TIME TO SHARE A GLIMPSE OF YOUR WORLD AND WORK WITH OUR READERS. PLEASE INTRODUCE YOURSELF. WHO IS NICOLLETTE SULLIVAN?

Nicollette Sullivan: Thank you for having me, I am so appreciative and honored! Haha, that's a question I'm still learning the answer to everyday. What I know so far is, I'm just a creative soul from Venice, California expressing myself and channeling my passion through music. I also don't know if Myself and "Nicollette" are the same, don't get me wrong there are aspects of Nicollette which are completely me, but the way I look at it is she is like a character in a book or script that I'm writing and then going to play. The character is part myself but also an amalgamation of all the things I have been inspired by and have experienced. Nicollette is a timeless nymph who dances across the sky serenading all who will listen.

2. IN WHAT WAYS DID YOUR FORMATIVE YEARS SHAPE YOUR LIFE'S PERSPECTIVE?

Nicollette Sullivan: Aesthetically, I found a love of vintage movies as a kid, watching movies with my mother and grandmother, eventually on my own... Which has heavily inspired a lot of my work. Being mixed race, I have experienced some adversity that has also shaped the way I view the world now.

3. WHEN DID YOU FALL IN LOVE WITH THE WORLD OF MUSIC AND WHAT WERE SOME OF THE FACTORS THAT INSPIRED YOU TO PURSUE THIS AVENUE AS A CAREER?

Nicollette Sullivan: I have loved singing for as long as I can remember. I grew up around my parents who were both involved with music themselves. I was surrounded by talented musicians growing up so naturally I wanted to become one.

.

4. YOU ARE OFTEN NOTED FOR YOUR SEDUCTIVE STYLE OF SONG.
AS A MUSICAL ARTIST, WHO ARE SOME OF YOUR INFLUENCES?

Nicollette Sullivan: I have a vast variety of the music I like. Some artists that influence me are Billy Holiday, Ella Fitzgerald, Nina Simone, Peggy Lee, Julie London, Sarah Vaughan , Doris Day, Patsy Cline, Whitney Houston, Alicia Keys, Christina Aguilera, Mariah Carey, Arianna Grande......

5. AS A SONGWRITER, WHAT ARE SOME OF THE MESSAGES THAT YOU TRY TO INFUSE INTO YOUR MUSIC?

Nicollette Sullivan: On this first album I have a lot of darker subject matter but I have an array of messages in my music, I of course sing about love.... I'm holding a torch for someone or another in a lot of my music... Because the world just needs another love song haha.. I also like to infuse messages of self-love and inner peace.

6. HOW DID YOUR UPCOMING SINGLE SWEET. DREAMS COME INTO BEING?

Nicollette Sullivan: I always loved the song but knew that the song is such a classic I'd have to give it my own spin. So we came up with the version on my record. I couldn't have done it without the help of my producer Shamanesque and the incredible piano playing of Ed Roth who actually plays with Annie Lennox in her touring band, the brilliant horn arrangements of Lee Thornburg, and of course the saucy counterpoint vocals of Big Llou Johnson.

7. WHAT CAN AUDIENCES EXPECT TO HEAR ON YOUR NEW ALBUM "NICOLLETTE," WHICH IS SLATED FOR RELEASE ON MAY 21ST, 2021?

Nicollette Sullivan: Audiences can expect to be whisked away on a journey through time, across beautiful musical landscapes. Hopefully the album will take you through a myriad of emotions and feelings.

8. AS FAR AS BEING A WOMAN IN MUSIC, WHAT HAS CHANGED AND WHAT COULD BE DONE BETTER?

Nicollette Sullivan: I feel it is important as a young woman in a musical field that is largely male dominated is that I am heard and respected as an artist. I speak my mind and I stand up for my values and creative choices. While I respect and listen to others, I know that my voice is important and of value. And I would encourage any young woman getting into this field to honor their voice as well.

9. HOW CAN FANS OF NICOLLETTE SULLIVAN'S MUSIC KEEP UP WITH YOUR LATEST PROGRESS AND EVENTS SURROUNDING YOUR WORK? ANY FINAL THOUGHTS?

Nicollette Sullivan: Anyone who wants to stay notified should go to my website **www.nicollettesullivan.com** and follow me on social media **@nicollettesullivan** on Instagram where you can also find links to all my social platforms.

As far as final thoughts are concerned, I'd just say to all my fans stay true to your soul's passion, never let anyone get you down and keep putting one foot in front of the other on your life's journey. And be thankful for everything in your life.

NICOLETTE SULLIVAN

OVER-SEXUALIZATION
OF FEMALE ARTISTS

In an industry where women make up only 28 percent of the publishing and record label workforce, female artists often struggle to gain credibility and success. When the growing fantasy of a hyper-sexualized world is thrown in the mix, it's no surprise that women are often portrayed as objects rather than people. In today's society, most women are expected to rely on their appearance to be successful. Most of the pressures that they face come from the male-dominated nature of the industry; however, some prominent female artists are doing more harm than good in combating these issues.

From Miley Cyrus to Nicki Minaj, some number of women have willingly put their bodies on display to capture their audiences' attention. One female artist who's rapid rise to fame is due in part to her sexualized image is Cardi B. To be fair, Cardi had a sexualized image before she started producing music. It wasn't just a byproduct of the pressure experienced within the industry.

SEXUALIZATION IN MUSIC VIDEOS

It seems that music videos lately accumulate the top views through the sexualization of women and their bodies. This action has been repeated consistently and not questioned in society, thus resulting in this sexualization culture to be accepted. Oversexualization in music videos is problematic because it can and has negatively impacted the self-esteem of many women.

Many current mainstream music videos contain lots of salacious lyrics and sexualization of women. Women are portrayed with "close-ups pouting lips, wiggling bottoms, shimmying cleavages and bare, toned stomachs feature heavily too", thus emphasizing a certain unrealistic look for many women to feel pressured to achieve in order to feel attractive (Dove 2018). Music videos contain sexualization because this is what captures an audience and creates the most revenue for the artist. Unfortunately, due to the focus on wealth, music videos fail to recognize how its imagery can
negatively affect any viewer.

For instance, based on a study done by the American Psychological Society, "girls who are exposed to sexualized content are more likely to endorse gender stereotypes and place attractiveness as central to a woman's value" (Coulson 2014). Additionally, boys who are constantly exposed to sexualized content, such as music videos, create unrealistic expectations of women and have a higher chance of sexually harassing women (Coulson 2014).

A common counter to the sexualized music videos is that the portrayal of sexualized women is intended to empower women and feel liberated in expressing their sexuality; however, "the reality is that often these women and their actions are managed and directed by men" (Lodhi 2016). Another problematic issue with sexualized women in music videos is the double standard for women and men in these videos. Many male artists that partake in this culture tend to dress in casual or formal wear, while the women in the videos are wearing little to no clothes. This commonly used concept reinforces the "male sexual fantasy and portray a masculine-ordered beauty imperative [and] are so only as part of a bigger patriarchal superstructure" (Burbidge 2015).

Paternalism, the idea of those who have power maintain their power and diminish the power of their subordinate, can be seen in music videos. The music industry and society celebrates and places higher value on videos with the most views. Coincidentally, the most views are obtained through the hypersexualization of women in music videos.

WOMEN
IN THE MUSIC INDUSTRY

Even taking into account the impact of the pandemic, it has never been a better time for independent creators in the music business. The various 2020 lockdowns may have prevented artists from earning vital touring income and disrupted release and promotion cycles, but for many it also pushed new creativity, with nearly 70% of independent artists choosing to use the time to write or make new music.

Yet, with access to the industry easier than ever, a glaring discrepancy remains: why are there still so few women, and so many men? What is stopping female creators – artists, songwriters, producers and DJs from picking up an instrument or learning the software, and releasing music into the market? Despite women occupying leadership positions and topping the charts, women overall remain starkly in the minority and remain massively unrepresented in the music industry. Why?

Hanna Kahlert

The challenges women and others face in the music industry (and beyond) are deep, varied and unrelenting – some obvious and now exposed (in part through #metoo), but many either subtle or deniable enough to have escaped accountability for decades, if not centuries. #metoo shone the spotlight on harassment and assault, often by men in positions of power. Yet discrimination and bias can also be as simple as girls experiencing discouragement from participating in "male" activities in schools, like technology, or from playing 'male' instruments likes drums and guitar.

t's well known that women creators in the music industry (and other sectors too) must work harder to achieve the same approval or reward as their male counterparts. They are sometimes treated with an air of dismissal, or are not as initially respected, or suffer expectations of childcare/parenthood as a burden or skill proclivity based on gender.

Much has been done over the past few years to address a myriad of these issues in music by the likes of Women In Live Music (WILM), Women In CTRL, Pass the Aux and more. The F-List female creator database has removed the excuse that there simply "aren't enough women in music to hire". Female-centric projects like Rhythm Sister, She Is the Music and SheShreds are working to develop, provide resources for and spotlight female artists that both inspire and empower the journeys of more women and other minorities into music.

The Annenberg Study highlighted shocking statistics, finding that only one-in-five of artists are female, but worse: only 12.3% of songwriters and 2.1% of producers are (2012-2018). While men and women of colour have climbed ladders, and female representation in the 'big leagues' is rising, behind the scenes it remains to be seen how much has really changed. No in-depth work has recently consulted the global community of female creators. This, too, is changing. MIDiA has long focused on the path of the independent artist, and in conjunction with Tunecore and Believe Digital we are now conducting a comprehensive global study asking creators themselves about their challenges, inspirations and experiences.

BOOKS
ABOUT WOMEN WHO CHANGED THE WORLD
Stories about women who stood up, spoke out, struggled through, and soared.

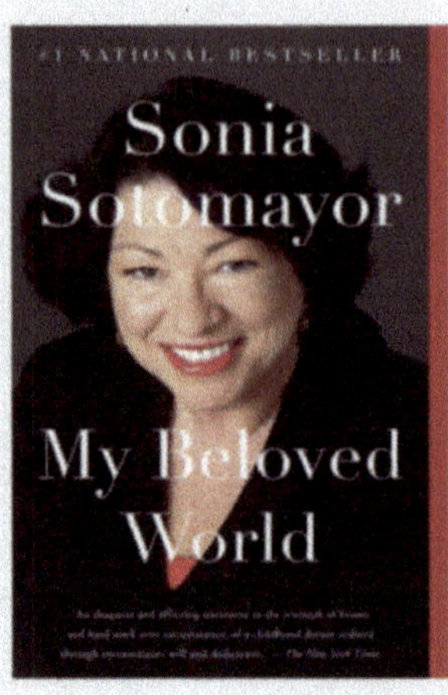

MY BELOVED WORLD
by Sonia Sotomayor

The first Hispanic and third woman appointed to the United States Supreme Court, Sonia Sotomayor has become an instant American icon. Now, with a candor and intimacy never undertaken by a sitting Justice, she recounts her life from a Bronx housing project to the federal bench, a journey that offers an inspiring testament to her own extraordinary determination and the power of believing in oneself.
Available from:
Amazon-Barnes & Noble-Books A Million-Bookshop.org

FINDING MY VOICE
by Valerie Jarrett

"The ultimate Obama insider" (The New York Times) and longest-serving senior advisor in the Obama White House shares her journey as a daughter, mother, lawyer, business leader, public servant, and leader in government at a historic moment in American history.

Available from:
Amazon-Barnes & Noble-Books A Million-Bookshop.org

KNOW MY NAME
by Chanel Miller

Know My Name will forever transform the way we think about sexual assault, challenging our beliefs about what is acceptable and speaking truth to the tumultuous reality of healing. It also introduces readers to Chanel Miller, an extraordinary writer, one whose words have already changed our world. Entwining pain, resilience, and humor, this memoir will stand as a modern classic

Available from:
Amazon-Barnes & Noble-Books A Million-Bookshop.org

No One Is Too Small to Make a Difference Deluxe Edition
by Greta Thunberg
The groundbreaking speeches of Greta Thunberg, the young climate activist who has become the voice of a generation, including her historic address to the United Nations.

BOOKS
ABOUT WOMEN WHO CHANGED THE WORLD

Stories about women who stood up, spoke out, struggled through, and soared.

WE SHOULD ALL BE FEMINISTS

by Chimamanda Ngozi Adichie

Chimamanda Ngozi Adichie offers readers a unique definition of feminism for the twenty-first century, one rooted in inclusion and awareness. Drawing extensively on her own experiences and her deep understanding of the often masked realities of sexual politics, here is one remarkable author's exploration of what it means to be a woman now—and an of-the-moment rallying cry for why we should all be feminists.
Available from:
Amazon-Barnes & Noble-Books A Million-Bookshop.org

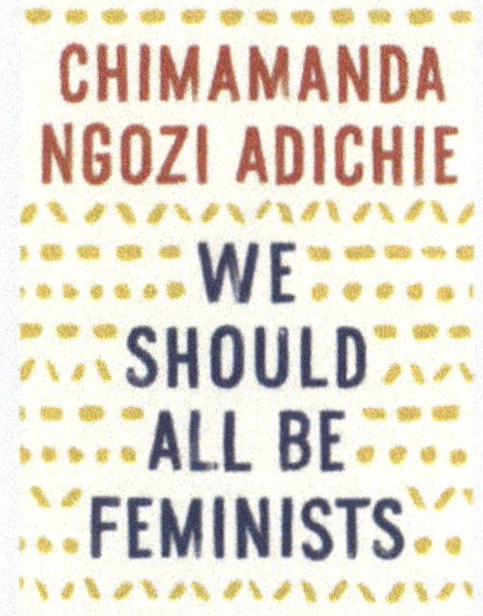

Things I've Been Silent About
by Azar Nafisi

In this stunning personal story of growing up in Iran, Azar Nafisi shares her memories of living in thrall to a powerful and complex mother against the backdrop of a country's political revolution.

Available from:
Amazon-Barnes & Noble-Books A Million-Bookshop.org

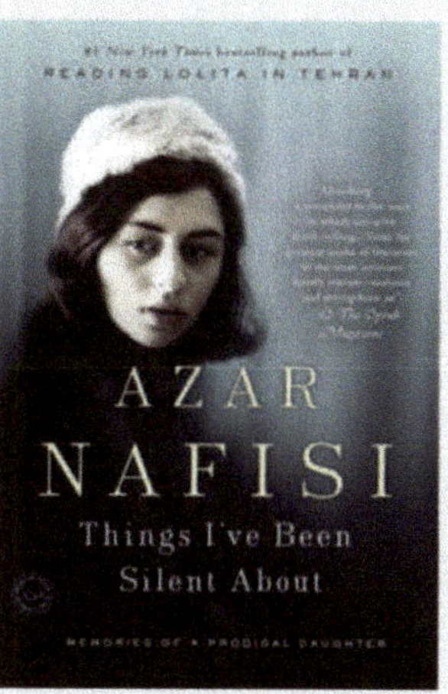

HEADSTRONG
by Rachel Swaby

Covering Nobel Prize winners and major innovators, as well as lesser-known but hugely significant scientists who influence our every day, Rachel Swaby's vibrant profiles span centuries of courageous thinkers and illustrate how each one's ideas developed, from their first moment of scientific engagement through the research and discovery for which they're best known. This fascinating tour reveals 52 women at their best—while encouraging and inspiring a new generation of girls to put on their lab coats.

Available from:
Amazon-Barnes & Noble-Books A Million-Bookshop.org

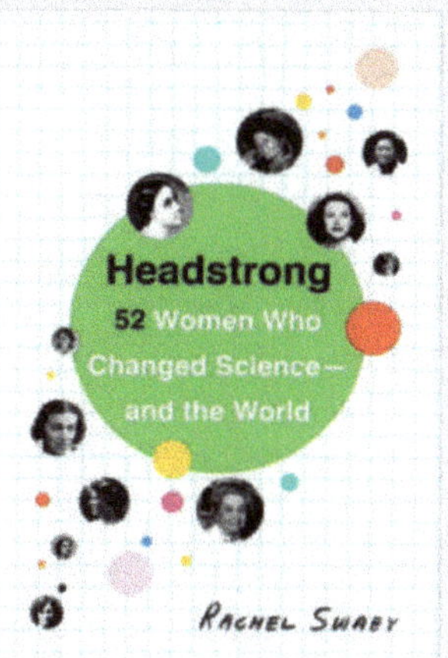

TOP WOMEN INDIE ARTISTS

"LOVE IS CALLING" BY SARA ROSE WASSON
An inspiring song that expresses faith in the strength of love!

Sara Rose Wasson is s a beautiful songstress with a distinct taste of voice a spirited presence as a performer. The Los Angeles-native grew up in the entertainment industry, but as an adult pursued different career endeavors, anything from permaculture farming to taking care of people's children, grandparents, animals, and businesses before rediscovering of her first love, music. In 2021, Sara Rose Wasson unveils the dexterity of her talent within the new single Love Is Calling.

Love Is Calling is an enthusiastic melody that embodies elements of pop, r&b, and soul into its structure for the creation of an exotic sound. The song begins with smoothing measures of piano and synth accompanied by Sara's refreshing voice. As the track progresses, other instruments begin to fill the room, which gives the production a feeling of ascent. An alluring rhythm from the electric guitar and the crisp pictorial drumming gives this production a tremendous air of warmth and transcendence.

Sara Rose Wasson successfully transports the listener into a whirlpool of inspiration with her spirited performance in song. Love Is Calling is an inspiring song that expresses faith in the strength of love and its transformative properties. Sara's message and admonishment is clear in the song's lyricism and the hope of "love greeting you with open arms" makes the subject of love's richness palatable for those searching for this life-rewarding experience and acts as a confirmation for many who are in love.
www.SaraRoseWasson.com

SAY WHAT YOU MEAN (REMIXES) BY EM

Remixed by Grammy award-winning producer Jared Gosselin, Say What You Mean takes on a different view of Em's artistry and performance. Say What You Mean's Wonder Urban Mix explores a seductive process through sound. The track possesses a clever sparsity that directs our attention to Em's vocal tone and range, thereby place her performance at the center stage of our minds. Draped in the essence of serenity, the Wonder Urban Mix utilizes jazz guitar, an unorthodox drum pattern, handclaps, and synth to unlock Em's theme of truth wrapped within romanticism.

The Wonder X Remix of Say What You Mean is a bit more theatrical than its preceding versions and takes on a wonderful EDM landscape and approach for the creation of a lovely dance tune. The listener gets to hear more of Em's vocal arrangements, harmonies, and overdubs that are intricately-woven into the groove's stride. The track's unique musical terrain emphasizes Em's modern execution of the song's theme, which is enlivened by measures of synth and a melodic drum kit for a fabulous experience that can be had at home or the dancefloor.

The remixes for Say what You Mean successfully maximizes the melody's potential while expounding upon the depth of Em's talent and creativity. It is simple a trip to the stars from here. Say What You Mean by Em is the first destination along the way.

Elegant songstress Aneessa,
is preparing the official release of her latest album
"SATISFIED"
produced by Michael B. Sutton – which is set to drop on the 26th of March.

The construction of the album, not to mention the individual songs, are infused with patience and diligence. This patience is on display immediately in the opening title track – a cover of the epic hit **"Back To Life (However Do You Want Me)"**, originally recorded by Soul II Soul. It fades in, gentle and languid, offering an introduction that meticulously avoids excessive bombast.

A smooth rolling beat and an emotive sax introduces Aneessa, who demonstrates the nuance and control she has in her voice before she slides to the front of the mix. And then, when Aneessa herself finally does step into the spotlight, we hear a voice that evokes passion and poignancy. The mellow but rhythmic backdrop is perfect for her tone, painting images of smoke-obscured clubs and black-tie fashion. It's a stunning start.

"Just To Be With You" forges an evocative melody, on top of a smooth jazz rhythm, as Aneessa unfolds the complications and afflictions of couples who are involved in long distance love, interracial experiences, or different religious faiths. Alongside a voice that switches effortlessly from low to high register, we can once again savor the resonating sax notes and the bubbling basslines. For all the conventional maturity on display, there is also a sense of exploration here.

"Saint-Etienne" is a very personal and affecting song about Aneessa's hometown in France. Here she unpacks her youthful dreams and painful memories describing why she eventually decided to leave that part of her life behind her. The super cool arrangement and expansive organic instrumentation, featuring Latin percussion and acoustic guitar motifs, generates a sense of bittersweet nostalgia.

Aneessa with music producer and husband Michael B. Sutton

Aneessa with background singer and vocal arranger Dionyza - and music producer/husband Michael B. Sutton

Aneessa's accomplished performances weaves tales of love, loss, self-doubt, discovery and empowerment, across an album of highly polished music.

Aneessa's voice is a rare gift; powerful, seductive and enthralling.
But it's not her voice alone that makes her exceptional though,
it is Aneessa's versatility that truly sets her apart.
This album weaves between styles and tempos, never stopping for breath.

"I Found Myself in You" slows things down to a love ballad, in a duet with singer-songwriter Michael B. Sutton. Skillfully arranged, the two step out into the unknown, over pianos and acoustic guitars, crafting a sound and vibe that is sincerely theirs. The title track "Satisfied", comes from the pen of Michael B. Sutton and his first wife Brenda. Their daughter Tiffany, suggested that Aneessa should record the song, resulting in an excellent proposal.

Aneessa makes "Satisfied" completely her own, as she showcases a provocative and sultry tone over a funky mid-tempo beat. And when she introduces some French language interludes, you can slowly dim the lights, as Aneessa's voice aims straight for your heart, regardless of what she's singing. "Miles Away" is Aneessa's personal take on the Madonna song, which she gives a more intimate and fluid workover.

Aneessa - www.aneessa.com

"Dream A Little Dream of Me" originally written by Fabian Andre and Wilbur Schwandt, and released in 1931, again sees Aneessa fearlessly take on a classic song. Subtly driven at its core, by the piano and a ukulele, the song expands into a rich theatrical ShowTime sound, with a blues twist and a jazz guitar solo. All of which brings us to the elegant dancefloor groove of "Gonna Be Alright". She often reaches intoxicating tones with her vocal in such a way that she seems to have completely given herself over to song.

The album closes with Aneesa's cover of the classic, cheeky Christmas song "Santa Baby", written by Joan Javits, Phil Springer, and Tony Springer. She does two versions – one in English, and the other in French.
Throughout these 10 songs, Aneessa commands a mastery of various styles, with enough covers and originals to flesh out a varied, captivating album.

Any indulgences are offset by her raw talent and singular moments that define her sound. "Satisfied" is the sound of a true talent who's already found herself. She is now stepping forward with complete control of her vision.

Produced by Michael B. Sutton - Lead Vocals : Aneessa - Background Vocals : Dionyza, Aneessa
Musicians: Drums: James Gadson-Keyboards: Hiroshi Upshur, Michael B. Sutton, Michael Norfleet
Percussion: Timbali Cornwell - Guitar: Josh Sklair, Tommy O - Bass: James Manning -
Saxophone: Fernando Harkless.
Mixing Engeneers: Jason Ruch - Jason Anderson
CD Mastered by James Forbes
Label: The Sound of L.A. www.TheSoundofLA.com

To now more about Aneessa, please visit: www.aneessa.com
Follow Aneessa on social media @AneessaMusic
Pre-Order Aneessa's new album "Satisfied" - www.aneessa.com

L.A. UNLIMITED

APPAREL REPRESENTATION
WITHOUT LIMITS...

- Corporate Brand Representation
- Brand Identity & Management
- Brand Consulting
- Trade Show Preparation & Participation
- Trunk Shows
- Private Label Sales
- Production Sourcing

L.A. Unlimited & Associates
30765 Pacific Coast Hwy STE
443Malibu, CA 90265

310.882.6432
sales@launlimitedinc.com

SPRING 2021
MUST-HAVE FASHION

As we go back in time with fashion, lots of the new spring 2021 trends are inspired by our favorite decades. Today, I will share three pieces that you need to add in your wardrobe to stay stylish.

FANTASY FLORALS

Flowers, which signify new beginnings, peppered the runways at Rodarte (photo),

Anna Sui, and Erdem. Some designers took an all-over approach by mixing florals head-to-toe.

BIRDS OF A FEATHER

We'd all love to spread our wings and take flight at this moment in time, but for now, a feathered skirt—perhaps in purple—will have to do the trick.

Whether layered with puffers à la Fendi (photo) or worn with chunky knit sweaters, the feather trend has fully taken off.

BEST OF BRA

Undergarments that promote function are one thing, but making a midriff-baring fashion statement are what spring 2021's bras are all about.

Go for matchy-matchy like Dolce did or try a cheeky twist on "business-casual" as seen at Tom Ford and Rosetta Getty.

READ MORE
ON
WWW.PUMPITUPMAGAZINE.COM

TEESPRING.COM/STORES/CHIARAMASERATI
ChiaraMaserati
ROLLERSKATE
GIRLY
COLLECTION
THIS IS HOW I
ROLL
THIS IS HOW I
ROLL
Tote Bag
$19.99:
DON'T HATE
Rollerskate
Various tee-shirts in all
colors
$22.99

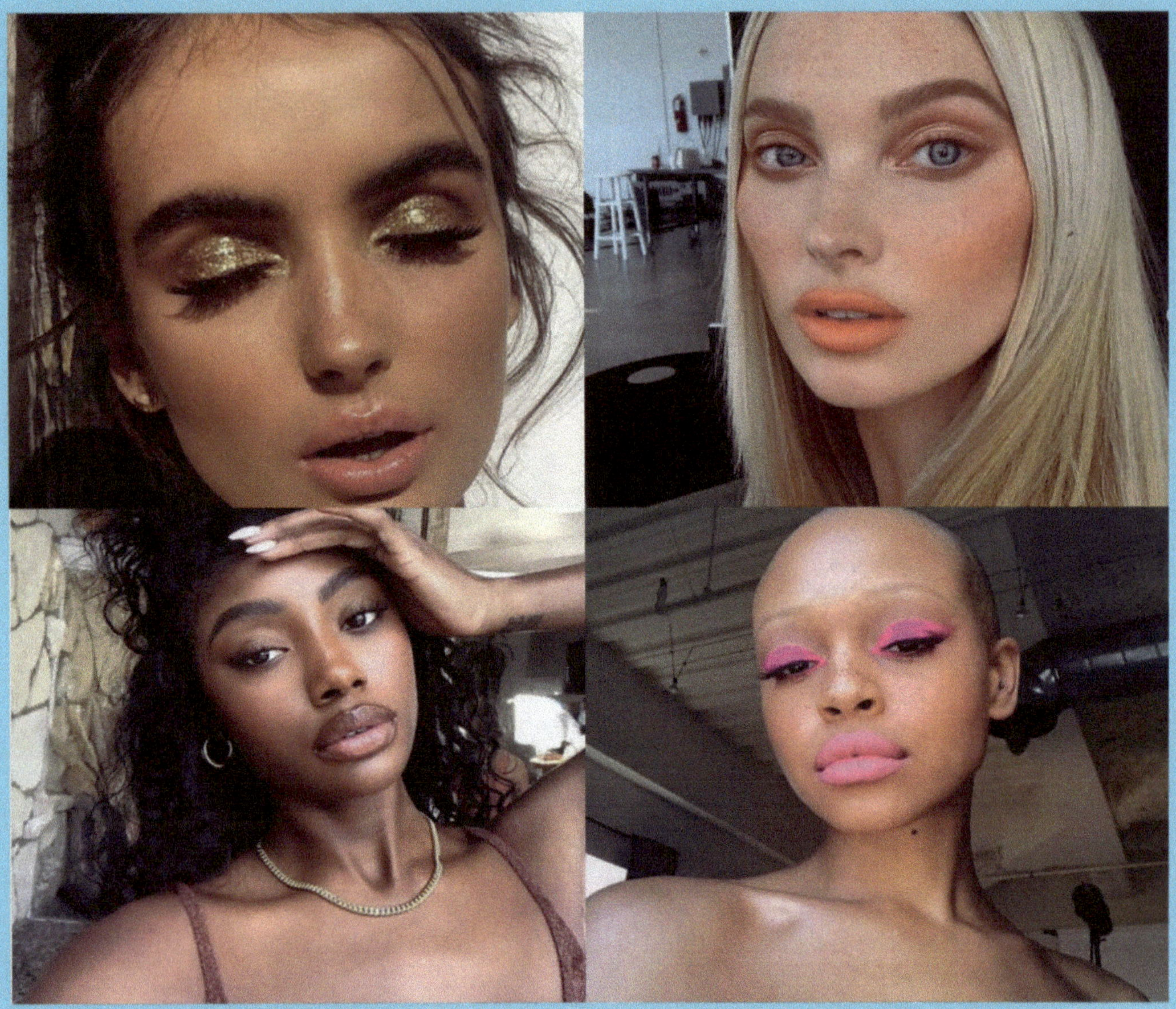

SPRING 2021 MAKE-UP TRENDS

THIS YEAR'S SPRING MAKEUP TRENDS
ARE ALL ABOUT COLOR—THINK:
VIBRANT PINK LIPSTICK AND
SHIMMERY GOLD EYESHADOW.

SPRING 2021
MAKE-UP TRENDS
Makeup Trends That You'll Want to Wear Year-Round

SMOLDERING EYELINERS

With all of the mask wearing in our future, Stern predicts smoldering eye looks will reign supreme among the 2021 makeup trend set.

"A classic, wet-lined liner look can really make us feel put-together," she explains. "I'm obsessed with Jillian Dempsey's Khòl Eyeliners ($20). They're clean, and they come in all colors."

SKY-HIGH LASHES

Undoubtedly, 2021 will be the year for everything eyes and lashes, and Stern says the longer and more lifted, the better where your flutter is concerned.

She cites lash lifts (versus extensions) as an up-and-coming trend surge as far as splurge-worthy treatments go. "This is a super-easy and accessible way to have a major beauty look with minimum effort," says Stern. "Look for technicians in your neighborhood and make sure that you read their customer reviews!"

LIPS - RESURGENCE OF EARLY 2000S

 The key, however, is to keep things light and fresh. To try the look yourself, Loiz recommends filling in your brows with light, upward strokes using a thin brow pencil, which ensures a more realistic finish that mimics your natural brow hairs.

Then, create your chocolatey brown lip by outlining your pout with a flesh-tone lip liner, filling it all in with a moisturizing lipstick, and pressing your lips together to blur out the lip line. She suggests shopping Propa Beauty's collection of lipstick, which contains a wide variety of neutral brown hues that cater to all skin tones.er of Color May Vary, a Black-owned beauty guide.

DELIT FACE

Social Media For The Entertainment World

MUSIC & MOVIE Industry

SINGER
SONGWRITER
MUSICIANS
PRODUCERS
PUBLISHERS
DISTRIBUTORS
MUSIC SUPERVISORS

ACTORS
DIRECTORS
PRODUCERS
DISTRIBUTORS
SET DESIGNERS
SCRIPT
WRITERS
EXTRAS

MAKE UP ARTISTS
HAIR STYLISTS
PHOTOGRAPHERS
GRAPHIC DESIGNER

Register now FREE and connect with people in your industry
www.delitface.com

"When you fall in love you are hesitant t o say what your heart feels, so I expressed it in a song"
Those Words
MICHAEL B. SUTTON
Spotify amazon iTunes
TIDAL
IN STORES NOW

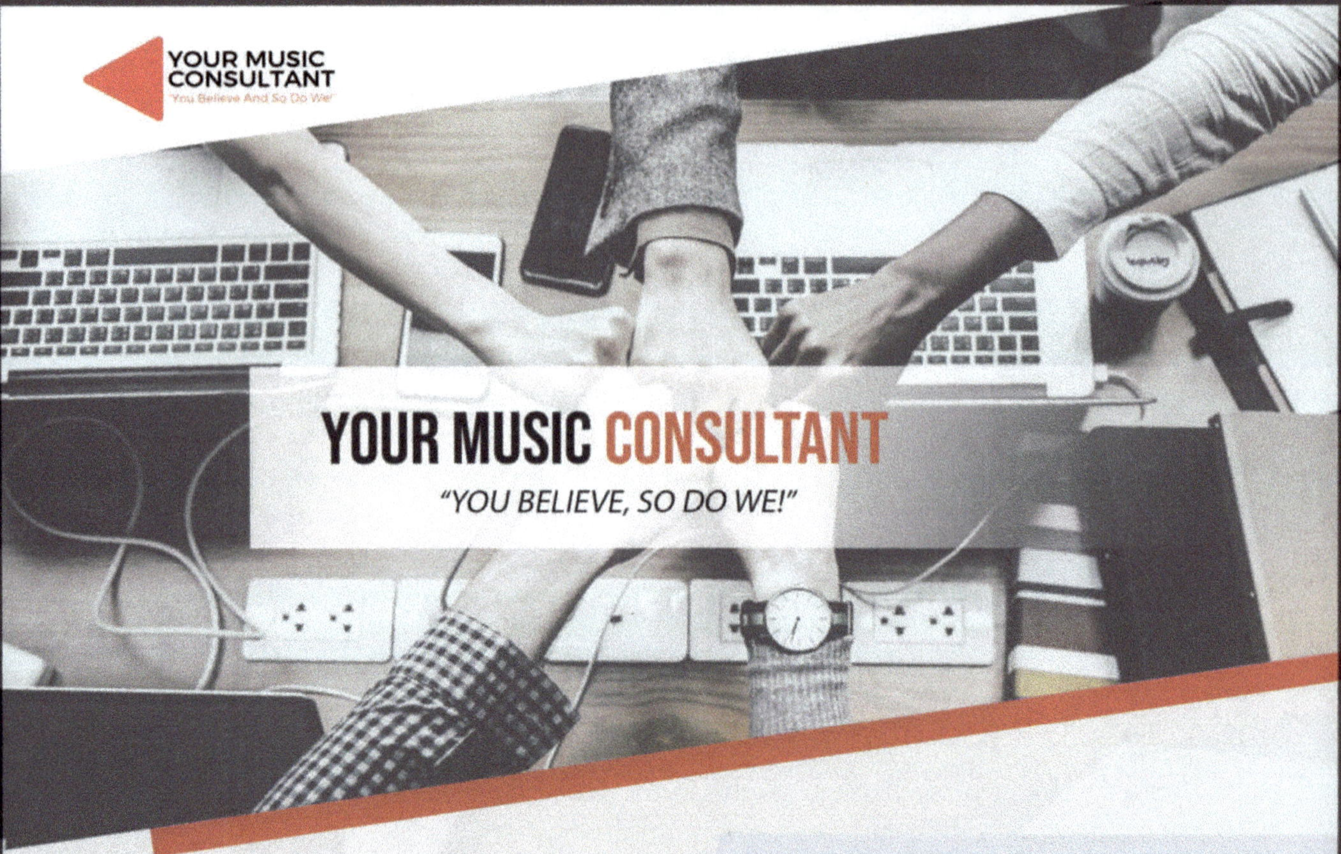

We Can Help You To Grow Your Business

We are a monthly based service, we put faith in artists who has major potential, believed in them, and who are willing to spend their time and own money to work with us in building a successful music career!

Digital Marketing Services

SOCIAL MEDIA - STREAMING SERVICES - MUSIC DISTRIBUTION - PRESS RELEASE - PRESS DISTRIBUTION - PR

Radio Airplay and TV Commercial

TERRESTRIAL AND DIGITAL RADIO CAMPAIGN AL GENRES EXCEPT HEAVY METAL - CABLE TV AND MAJOR NETWORK COMMERCIAL

Licensing & Booking

CONCERTS, LIVE MUSIC, EVENTS, CLUB NIGHTS - RED CARPETS - FOREIGN LICENSING AND SUBPUBLISHING

Why Choose Us ?

3 DECADES OF MUSIC BUSINESS EXPERIENCE
Platinium and Gold Records
MOTOWN RECORDS
UNIVERSAL
SONY
CAPITOL RECORDS

WE WORKED WITH:
Kanye West - Jay Z - Stevie Wonder - Michael Jackson - Germaine Jackson Smokey Robinson - Dionne Warwick - Cheryl Lynn - The Originals -

1 -818-514-0038 (Ext. 1)
Monday - Friday / 9am to 6pm

FIND US :

www.YourMusicConsultant.com
30721 Russell Ranch Road Suite 140 Westlake Village, USA
Email : info@yourmusicconsultant.com

"PHATT"
IN STORES NOW
DRIVETIME
Phatt
JAZZ BAND DRIVETIME
IS BACK
WITH A HOT NEW
URBAN ORGANIC FUNK
JOINT"PHATT"
PLEASE VISIT:
WWW.DRIVETIMEUOJ.COM

TOP
TIPS

MAKING
A LIVING
WITH YOUR MUSIC

HOW TO MAKE A LIVING
WITH YOUR MUSIC

Do you need to "know somebody" or "get lucky" to build a fan base and grow an income as an artist?
Absolutely not!

BUILD AN EMAIL LIST.

Here's what I did… and what I recommend YOU do if you want to grow a fan base and grow an income. It's really a simple process. Grow an email list full of fans, and build a genuine relationship with them over time. Then invite them to buy your songs.

MAKE FRIENDS WITH YOUR NEW SUBSCRIBERS.

Be genuine. Be real. Be open. Be honest.
Give them an insider's look into your process. Tell them real stories about the real you. Don't disrespect them by hammering them with nonstop sales messages!
Give them things they'd never get if they weren't on your list. Make them look forward to hearing from you! If you do these things, they will buy your music — even today, when they don't have to buy ANY music from ANYONE. Your "secret ninja weapon" is a genuine connection with your fans.

ADVERTISING

In the heyday of pop and rock, musicians rarely wanted to be associated with corporate brands, but that's changing with the rise of rap as America's most popular genre. Brand partnerships offer artists the ability to sponsor or endorse a brand they might genuinely like, and get access to an additional revenue stream while they're at it. Another way musicians find side money is from YouTube monetization, wherein YouTube videos share in the profit from the ads that come tagged onto them. Psy's "Gangnam Style" reportedly made $2 million from 2 billion YouTube views. YouTube's head of music Lyor Cohen wrote in a blog post last year that YouTube's payout rate in the U.S. is as high as $3 per 1000 streams.

FASHION, MERCHANDISING, AND OTHER DIRECT SELLS

Selling non-music products like perfumes, paraphernalia and clothing lines is an easy money-making strategy that artists have been taking advantage of for decades — but in the digital era, musicians can also get creative with their methods, expanding well beyond traditional merch tents at concerts and posters on a website.

Artists are also starting to ask for money from audiences directly — via crowdfunding or creating custom channels of communication with their fans — outside of social media platforms like Instagram and Twitter. The Voice star Angie Johnson raised roughly $36,000 on Kickstarter to record an upcoming album, for instance. More groups are releasing dedicated apps or subscription packages for their music or selling bespoke products like artist-curated festivals, email subscriptions and limited music releases. Pitbull has his own cruise.

STREAMING

The music industry has now accepted streaming as its revenue-leader and is poised to adapt around that, with many analysts and experts expecting that the business will streamline itself — with rewrites of law, new royalties negotiations, mergers, acquisitions and consolidations — into something leaner and, finally, more lucrative for musicians. Bad news: No one knows when that will be.

HER VOICE WOULD NOT BE SILENCED
ANDRA DAY
A LEE DANIELS FILM
A hulu ORIGINAL FILM
THE UNITED STATES VS.
BILLIE HOLIDAY
SCREENPLAY BY SUZAN-LORI PARKS DIRECTED BY LEE DANIELS

THE UNITED STATES VS. BILLIE HOLIDAY

In the 1940s, Billie Holiday is targeted by the government in an effort to racialize the war on drugs, ultimately aiming to stop her from singing her controversial song, "Strange Fruit."

The United States vs. Billie Holiday is a 2021 American biographical drama film about singer Billie Holiday, based on the book Chasing the Scream: The First and Last Days of the War on Drugs by Johann Hari. Directed by Lee Daniels, the film stars Andra Day in the titular role, along with Trevante Rhodes, Natasha Lyonne, and Garrett Hedlund.

Initially set to be theatrically released by Paramount Pictures, the film was sold to Hulu in December 2020, and digitally released in the United States on February 26, 2021. The United States vs. Billie Holiday received mixed reviews from critics, who praised Day's performance but criticized the direction and screenplay as unfocused. At the 78th Golden Globe Awards, it earned nominations for Best Actress – Motion Picture Drama (Day) and Best Original Song ("Tigress and Tweed").

Review aggregator Rotten Tomatoes reports that 56% of 98 critics gave the film a positive review, with an average rating of 5.4/10.
David Rooney of The Hollywood Reporter wrote: "Day mesmerizes even when Lee Daniels' unwieldy bio-drama careens all over the map with stylistic inconsistency and narrative dysfunction, settling for episodic electricity in the absence of a robust connective thread. It's a mess, albeit an absorbing one, driven by a raw central performance of blistering indignation, both tough and vulnerable."
Writing for Variety, Owen Gleiberman praised Day's performance and said, "In this sprawling, lacerating, but at times emotionally wayward biopic set during the last decade of Holiday's life, Day gives Billie a voice of pearly splendor that, over time, turns raspy and hard, and we see the same thing happening to Billie inside."

MINISTER PHYLLIS MCMEANS

"HELP"

A SONG OF HOPE
&
FAITH

PRE-ORDER NOW
IN STORES
FEBRUARY 12

WOMEN-LED MUSIC
ORGANIZATIONS YOU NEED TO JOIN

these amazing organizations are taking action to expedite equality and empower women to step up, fight back and support each other to build a better future for all of us. It's incredibly scary entering an industry with such a large gender gap, but women in all aspects of the industry are building a landscape for the future where this is no longer supported. These badass, women-led organizations are doing the most to do their part in changing the future of the music industry.
Check 'em out. Get involved. Do your part.

WOMEN IN MUSIC

Women in Music is an organization with a mission to advance the awareness, equality, diversity, heritage, opportunities, and cultural aspects of women in the musical arts through education, support, empowerment, and recognition.

Their countless events celebrate the female contribution to the music industry and aims to strengthen the ties between the two for a better future for women in music. WIM believes all voices are welcome in the conversation about equality.

By joining WIM, you'll get access to in-person networking and educational workshops all over the world, online networking groups, directories, newsletters, forums and more to help you directly interact with the WIM community. Additionally, WIM provides resources to thousands of women in need in various stages of their careers.

Please visit:
https://www.womeninmusic.org/

SHESAID.SO

Established back in 2014, shesaid.so is a global network of women in the music industry. Made up of women from record labels, bookings, artist management, tech, creative and more, this organization curates and speaks on panels discussing the importance of the movement with hopes to inspire anyone who will listen.

Additionally, shesaid.so challenges the industry's outdated framework with their Alternative Power 100 Music List and works towards increasing the number of women who progress in their careers with their mentoring program, she.grows.

"shesaid.so started as and continues to be a space where members can openly ask for advice, share jobs and events, announce new projects and build community. There are currently over 3,000 international members in the global community and an additional 10,000 members across our 15 local chapters."

Please visit:
https://www.shesaid.so/donate

CHANGE THE CONVERSATION

Founded by three successful music executives, Leslie Fram, Tracy Gershon and Beverly Keel, Change the Conversation fights gender inequality in the music industry by providing support, education and a community of like-minded female artists and executives all working towards the same goal of equality.

Please visit:
http://www.changetheconversation.net/connect

pre-order now
www.aneessa.com
ANEESSA
Satisfied